A Book of Very Short Poems

Say not the mermaid is a myth,
I knew one once named Mrs Smith.
She stood while playing cards or knitting:
Mermaids are not equipped for sitting.

This is a collection of very short poems, by all kinds of authors, on all sorts of subjects. From mermaids to bears, dragons to eggs, funny to serious, these short poems cover a lot of ground.

Michael Harrison was born in Oxford, and now lives there, having taught in North Queensland, London, Oxford, and Hartlepool. He is married, with two grown-up sons. His previous books include a history of witches, funny novels, retellings of Norse myths, and Don Quixote; numerous poetry anthologies in collaboration with Christopher Stuart-Clark; two novels for Oxford University Press: It's My Life and Facing the Dark; and a book of original poems, Junk Mail.

Other books in this series

Short!
A Book of Very Short Stories
Kevin Crossley-Holland

A Book of
Very Short
Poems

Collected by
Michael Harrison

OXFORD
UNIVERSITY PRESS

OXFORD

UNIVERSITY PRESS

Great Clarendon Street, Oxford OX2 6DP

Oxford University Press is a department of the University of Oxford.
It furthers the University's objective of excellence in research, scholarship,
and education by publishing worldwide in

Oxford New York

Athens Auckland Bangkok Bogotá Buenos Aires
Cape Town Chennai Dar es Salaam Delhi Florence Hong Kong Istanbul
Karachi Kolkata Kuala Lumpur Madrid Melbourne Mexico City Mumbai
Nairobi Paris São Paulo Shanghai Singapore Taipei Tokyo Toronto Warsaw
with associated companies in Berlin Ibadan

Oxford is a registered trade mark of Oxford University Press
in the UK and in certain other countries

This selection and arrangement copyright © Michael Harrison 2001
First published 2001

Many of these poems appeared in Michael Harrison's collection *Splinters*,
now unavailable.

British Library Cataloguing in Publication Data available

ISBN 0-19-276253-2

1 3 5 7 9 10 8 6 4 2

Inside illustrations by Sarah Young

Typeset by Mike Brain Graphic Design Limited

Printed and bound in Great Britain by Biddles Ltd

www.biddles.co.uk

This collection
is in memory
of the Grannies,
mine, and my children's.

Contents

The Early Morning

The moon on the one hand, the dawn on the
    other:
The moon is my sister, the dawn is my brother.
The moon on my left hand and the dawn on my
    right.
My brother, good morning: my sister, good night.

HILAIRE BELLOC

Shadows

Chunks of night
Melt
In the morning sun.
One lonely one
Grows legs
And follows me
To school.

PATRICIA HUBBELL

Diary

Got up, went to school,
did homework, went to bed.

All that is net: life's
quick fish escaped.

M. J. WILSON

The Relief of Myopia

The blackboard's white turned dark; I
Turned stupid. Teachers noticed. The optician's
Jumbled alphabet foxed me. A load for my nose.
And sudden and beautiful eyebrows flared on faces.

U. A. FANTHORPE

When I Was Three

When I was three I had a friend
Who asked me why bananas bend,
I told him why, but now I'm four,
I'm not so sure . . .

RICHARD EDWARDS

Radish

The radish is
the only dish
that isn't flat
but spherical.

Eating small
green peas off it
could make you quite
hysterical.

N. M. BODECKER

A Sum

I give thee all, I can no more,
    Though small thy share may be:
Two halves, three thirds, and quarters four
    Is all I bring to thee.

LEWIS CARROLL

My Love For You

I know you little, I love you lots;
My love for you would fill ten pots,
Fifteen buckets, sixteen cans,
Three teacups, and four dishpans.

TRADITIONAL

Don't Care

Don't care was made to care,
Don't care was hung;
Don't care was put in the pot
And boiled till he was done.

TRADITIONAL

Season Song

Spring stirs slowly, shuffles, hops;
Summer dances close behind.
Autumn is a jostling crowd
but Winter creeps into your mind.

JUDITH NICHOLLS

March

A blue day,
a blue jay,
and a good beginning.
One crow, melting snow—
spring's winning!

ELIZABETH COATSWORTH

April Gale

The wind frightens my dog, but I bathe in it,
Sound, rush, scent of the spring fields.

My dog's hairs are blown like feathers askew,
My coat's a demon, torturing like life.

IVOR GURNEY

Spring

Spring
slips
silent
snowdrops
past winter's iron gate.

Then daffodils'
golden trumpets
sound:
Victory!

HUGO MAJER

Nature Poem

Skylark, what prompts your silver song
To fountain up and down the sky?

Beetles roast
With fleas on toast
And earthworm pie.

ADRIAN MITCHELL

Hailstorm in May

Strike, churl; hurl, cheerless wind, then; heltering
    hail
May's beauty massacre and wispèd wild clouds
    grow
Out on the giant air; tell summer No,
Bid joy back, have at the harvest, keep Hope pale.

GERARD MANLEY HOPKINS

Bee

You want to make some honey?
All right. Here's the recipe.
Pour the juice of a thousand flowers
Through the sweet tooth of a Bee.

X. J. KENNEDY

God Made the Bees

God made the bees,
    And the bees make honey.
The miller's man does all the work
    But the miller makes the money.

TRADITIONAL

The Tickle Rhyme

'Who's that tickling my back?' said the wall.
'Me,' said a small
Caterpillar. 'I'm learning
To crawl.'

IAN SERRAILLIER

14

Caterpillar's Lullaby

Your sleep will be
a lifetime
and all your dreams
rainbows.
Close your eyes
and spin yourself
a fairytale:
Sleeping Ugly,
Waking Beauty.

JANE YOLEN

Butterfly

Butterfly
Butterflies
Butterflown

SIMON FOREST

The Butterfly

A book of summer is the butterfly:
The print is small and hard to read,
The pages ruffle in the wind,
And when you close them up they die.

JOHN FULLER

Where Innocent Bright-Eyed Daisies Are

Where innocent bright-eyed daisies are,
With blades of grass between,
Each daisy stands up like a star
Out of a sky of green.

CHRISTINA ROSSETTI

Love Without Hope

Love without hope, as when the young bird-
    catcher
Swept off his tall hat to the squire's own daughter,
So let the imprisoned larks escape and fly
Singing about her head, as she rode by.

ROBERT GRAVES

The Nest

Four blue stones in this thrush's nest
I leave, content to make the best
Of turquoise, lapis lazuli
Or for that matter of the whole blue sky.

ANDREW YOUNG

The Blue Room

My room is blue, the carpet's blue,
The chairs are blue, the door's blue too.
A blue bird flew in yesterday,
I don't know if it's flown away.

RICHARD EDWARDS

If I Walked Straight Slap

If I walked straight slap
Headlong down the road
Toward the two-wood gap
Should I hit that cloud?

IVOR GURNEY

Through Frost and Snow

Through frost and snow and sunlight,
through rain and night and day
I go back to where I came from.
I pass all things, yet stay.

BRIAN PATTEN

At the Land's End

On the beach
as waves sigh
two figures stand.
On the beach
hand in hand
three shadows lie.

JOHN FENNIMAN

The Dog

The truth I do not stretch or shove
When I state the dog is full of love.
I've also proved, by actual test,
A wet dog is the lovingest.

OGDEN NASH

Our Dog Chasing Swifts

A border collie has been bred to keep
Order among those wayward bleaters, sheep.
Ours, in a sheepless garden, vainly tries
To herd the screaming black sheep of the skies.

U. A. FANTHORPE

Alley Cat

A bit of jungle in the street
He goes on velvet toes,
And slinking through the shadows, stalks
Imaginary foes.

ESTHER VALCK GEORGES

The Poet's Cat

My cat—
Pangur Ban—
and I
hunt all night.
He for mice
to lay at my feet,
Me for words
to lay on this page.

JOHN FENNIMAN
(BASED ON AN ANONYMOUS IRISH POEM)

Epitaph for a Good Mouser

Take, Lord, this soul of furred unblemished worth,
The sum of all I loved and caught on earth.
Quick was my holy purpose and my cause.
I die into the mercy of thy claws.

ANNE STEVENSON

The Greater Cats

The greater cats with golden eyes
Stare out between the bars.
Deserts are there, and different skies,
And night with different stars.

V. SACKVILLE-WEST

Little Fish

The tiny fish enjoy themselves
in the sea.
Quick little splinters of life,
their little lives are fun to them
in the sea.

D. H. LAWRENCE

Fly Away, Fly Away

Fly away, fly away over the sea,
Sun-loving swallow, for summer is done;
Come again, come again, come back to me,
Bringing the summer and bringing the sun.

CHRISTINA ROSSETTI

Owl

A figure cloaked in the dark of the eaves.
In the night's auditorium blue-black there is nothing.
And nothing within your stomach's radius of hunger.

Only you can outsit the moon.

GORDON MASON

The Fairy Ring

Here the horse-mushrooms make a fairy ring,
    Some standing upright and some overthrown,
A small Stonehenge, where heavy black slugs cling
    And bite away, like Time, the tender stone.

ANDREW YOUNG

Dandelions

Such brazen slatterns:
but later, white-haired, genteel.

GERDA MAYER

Fog

The fog comes
on little cat feet.

It sits looking
over harbor and city
on silent haunches
and then moves on.

CARL SANDBURG

The Sun and Fog Contested

The Sun and Fog contested
The Government of Day—
The Sun took down his yellow whip
And drove the Fog away.

EMILY DICKINSON

On Bonfire Night

On bonfire night
seeing a wigwam of planks
being burnt
and concerned
about its future
the nearby fence
looks tense

JOHN HEGLEY

Splinter

The voice of the last cricket
across the first frost
is one kind of goodbye.
It is so thin a splinter of singing.

CARL SANDBURG

The Christmas Spider

My fine web sparkles:
Indoor star in the roof's night
Over the baby.

MICHAEL RICHARDS

After Breakfast

I stop myself sliding a morsel
Of bacon fat into the bin.
It will do as a meal for the robin,
His legs are so terribly thin.

ROY FULLER

The Redbreast

The redbreast smoulders in the waste of snow:
His eye is large and bright, and to and fro
He draws and draws his slender threads of sound
Between the dark boughs and the freezing
    ground.

ANTHONY RYE

Gales

Weather buffets our houses in armour all night.
There is no sleep that is not a war with sound.
Morning is safer. A good view of the battleground.
And no roof that is not between light and light.

ANNE STEVENSON

Trees

The trees are shrieking
Their hands thrust up in fright
Like an army of bone-men on the hill
Stopped in their tracks and turned to skin and stone.

BERLIE DOHERTY

Conceit

I heard a winter tree in song.
Its leaves were birds, a hundred strong;
When all at once it ceased to sing
For every leaf had taken wing.

MERVYN PEAKE

From the Winter Wind

From the winter wind
a cold fly
came to our window
where we had frozen our noses
and warmed his feet on the glass

MICHAEL ROSEN

Snow Poem

Winter
morning.
Snowflakes
for breakfast.
The street
outside
quiet
as a
long
white
bandage.

ROGER MCGOUGH

Winter Wise

Walk fast in snow, in frost walk slow,
And still as you go tread on your toe;
When frost and snow are both together,
Sit by the fire, and spare shoe leather.

TRADITIONAL

Thaw

Over the land freckled with snow half-thawed
The speculating rooks at their nests cawed
And saw from elm-tops, delicate as flower of grass,
What we below could not see, winter pass.

EDWARD THOMAS

The Man in the Wilderness

The man in the wilderness asked of me,
How many strawberries grew in the sea?
I answered him as I thought good,
As many red herrings as grew in a wood.

ANON.

Infant Innocence

The Grizzly Bear is huge and wild;
He has devoured the infant child.
The infant child is not aware
He has been eaten by the bear.

A. E. HOUSMAN

The Toaster

A silver-scaled dragon with jaws flaming red
Sits at my elbow and toasts my bread.
I hand him fat slices, and then, one by one,
He hands them back when he sees they are done.

WILLIAM JAY SMITH

Three Wise Men of Gotham

Three wise men of Gotham,
They went to sea in a bowl,
And if the bowl had been stronger
My song had been longer.

ANON.

The Mermaid

Say not the mermaid is a myth,
I knew one once named Mrs Smith.
She stood while playing cards or knitting:
Mermaids are not equipped for sitting.

OGDEN NASH

I Saw Esau

I saw Esau sawing wood,
And Esau saw I saw him;
Though Esau saw I saw him saw,
Still Esau went on sawing.

ANON.

He Went to the Wood

He went to the wood and caught it,
He sat him down and sought it;
Because he could not find it,
Home with him he brought it.

TRADITIONAL

Poem To Answer The Question:
How Old Are Fleas?

Adam
Had 'em

TRADITIONAL

Lord Finchley

Lord Finchley tried to mend the Electric Light
Himself.
      It struck him dead: And serve him right!
It is the business of the wealthy man
To give employment to the artisan.

HILAIRE BELLOC

They Might Not Need Me

They might not need me—yet they might—
I'll let my heart be just in sight—
A smile so small as mine might be
Precisely their necessity.

EMILY DICKINSON

Lesson from a Sundial

Ignore dull days; forget the showers;
Keep count of only shining hours.

ANON.

And the Days Are Not Full Enough

And the days are not full enough
And the nights are not full enough
And life slips by like a field mouse
   Not shaking the grass.

EZRA POUND

Clockface

Hours pass
slowly as a snail
creeping between the grassblades
of the minutes.

JUDITH THURMAN

Beyond Words

That row of icicles along the gutter
Feels like my armoury of hate;
And you, you . . . you, you utter . . .
You wait.

ROBERT FROST

The Fall-Out

A quarrel is a pair of scissors
Scoring points that go too deep,
And with steel in their cold hearts
Two people cut each other to shreds.

SANDY BROWNJOHN

Choose

The single clenched fist lifted and ready,
Or the open asking hand held out and waiting.
Choose:
For we meet by one or the other.

CARL SANDBURG

The White Thought

I shall be glad to be silent, Mother, and hear you
    speak,
You encouraged me to tell too much, and my
    thoughts are weak,
I shall keep them to myself for a time, and when I
    am older
They will shine as a white worm shines under a
    green boulder.

STEVIE SMITH

In the Eggs

In the eggs
the chickens say,
'Don't count
your foxes
before
you're hatched.'

JOHN CORBEN

Happy Thought

The world is so full of a number of things,
I'm sure we should all be as happy as kings.

ROBERT LOUIS STEVENSON

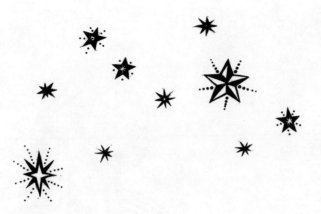

Bravado

Have I not walked without an upward look
Of caution under stars that very well
Might not have missed me when they shot and
    fell?
It was a risk I had to take—and took.

ROBERT FROST

No Lake Is So Still

No lake is so still but that it has its wave;
No circle so perfect but that it has its blur.
I would change things for you if I could;
As I can't, you must take them as they are.

OLD CHINESE RHYMING PROVERB
(TRANSLATED BY ARTHUR WALEY)

Good Appetite

Of breakfast, then of walking to the pond;
Of wind, work, rain, and sleep I never tire.
God of monotony, may you be fond
Of me and these forever, and wood fire.

MARK VAN DOREN

Ease

Lined coat, warm cap, and easy felt slippers,
In the little tower, at the low window, sitting over
    the sunken brazier.
Body at rest, heart at peace; no need to rise early.
I wonder if the courtiers at the Western Capital
    know of these things, or not?

PO CHU-I
(835 AD TRANSLATED FROM THE CHINESE BY ARTHUR
WALEY)

Be Like the Bird

Be like the bird, who
Resting in his flight
On a twig too slight
Feels it bend beneath him,
Yet sings
Knowing he has wings.

VICTOR HUGO

The Parent

Children aren't happy with nothing to ignore,
And that's what parents were created for.

OGDEN NASH

Eternity

He who binds to himself a joy
Does the winged life destroy;
But he who kisses the joy as it flies
Lives in eternity's sun rise.

WILLIAM BLAKE

The Tin Frog

I have hopped, when properly wound up, the
    whole length
Of the hallway; once hopped halfway down the
    stairs, and fell.
Since then the two halves of my tin have been
    awry; my strength
Is not quite what it used to be; I do not hop so
    well.

RUSSELL HOBAN

What Are Heavy?

What are heavy? Sea-sand and sorrow;
What are brief? Today and Tomorrow;
What are frail? Spring blossoms and youth;
What are deep? The ocean and truth.

CHRISTINA ROSSETTI

The Secret Sits

We dance round in a ring and suppose,
But the Secret sits in the middle and knows.

ROBERT FROST

I Give You

I give you the end of a golden string;
    Only wind it into a ball,
It will lead you in at Heaven's gate,
    Built in Jerusalem's wall.

WILLIAM BLAKE

From Prison

You took away all the oceans and all the room.
You gave me my shoe-size in earth with bars
    around it.
Where did it get you? Nowhere.
You left me my lips, and they shape words, even
    in silence.

OSIP MANDELSTAM

(TRANSLATED BY CLARENCE BROWN AND W.S.MERWIN)

The Coming of Good Luck

So good luck came, and on my roof did light
Like noiseless snow, or as the dew of night:
Not all at once, but gently, as the trees
Are by the sunbeams tickled by degrees.

ROBERT HERRICK

In Memoriam
(Easter, 1915)

The flowers left thick at nightfall in the wood
This Eastertide call into mind the men
Now far from home, who, with their sweethearts
    should
Have gathered them and will never do again.

EDWARD THOMAS

Summer Grasses

Summer grasses,
all that remains
of soldiers' dreams.

BASHO
(TRANSLATED FROM THE JAPANESE BY LUCIEN STRYK)

Napoleon

'What is the world, O Soldiers?
    It is I:
I, this incessant snow,
    This northern sky;
Soldiers, this solitude
    Through which we go
    Is I.'

WALTER DE LA MARE

65

Here Dead Lie We

Here dead lie we because we did not choose
To live and shame the land from which we sprung.
Life, to be sure, is nothing much to lose;
But young men think it is, and we were young.

A. E. HOUSMAN

A Maltese Dog

He came from Malta; and Eumêlus says
He had no better dog in all his days.
We called him Bull; he went into the dark.
Along those roads we cannot hear him bark.

TYMNES
(2ND CENTURY BC TRANSLATED FROM THE GREEK BY
EDMUND BLUNDEN)

Solitary Observation Brought Back from a Sojourn in Hell

At midnight tears
Run into your ears.

LOUISE BOGAN

In the Graveyard

The dead say, It is
not as we were told; their stones,
exclamation marks.

JOHN FENNIMAN

Harlech Castle

Here, decayed, an old
Giant's molar. It ground men's
Bones; their blood its bread.

JOHN CORBEN

Selling Home

Walking through the house,
now empty, echoing, life gone,
I look into my mother's mirror:
all that is left of her stares back.

MICHAEL RICHARDS

The Warning

Just now,
Out of the strange
Still dusk . . . as strange as still . . .
A white moth flew.
Why am I grown so cold?

ADELAIDE CRAPSEY

Small Rains

Bedtime tears
and evening sorrow,
here today
and gone tomorrow.

Small rains that pass
and passing cry:
'How-do-you-do?
Goodbye, goodbye.'

N. M. BODECKER

Good Night

Here's a body—there's a bed!
There's a pillow—here's a head!
There's a curtain—here's a light!
There's a puff—and so good night!

THOMAS HOOD

And So to Bed

'Night-night, my precious!'; 'Sweet dreams, sweet!'
'Heaven bless you, child!'—the accustomed grown-
    ups said.
Two eyes gazed mutely back that none could meet,
Then turned to face Night's terrors overhead.

WALTER DE LA MARE

Prayer

Grant that no Hobgoblins fright me,
No hungry devils rise up and bite me;
No Urchins, Elves, or drunkard Ghosts
Shove me against walls or posts.

JOHN DAY

Night Lights

There is no need to light a night-light
On a light night like tonight;
For a night-light's light's a slight light
When the moonlight's white and bright.

ANON.

Above the Dock

Above the quiet dock in midnight,
Tangled in the tall mast's corded height,
Hangs the moon. What seemed so far away
Is but a child's balloon, forgotten after play.

T. E. HULME

Others

'Mother, oh, mother! where shall we hide us?
Others there are in the house beside us—
Moths and mice and crooked brown spiders!'

JAMES REEVES

A Baby-Sermon

The lightning and thunder
    They go and they come;
But the stars and the stillness
    Are always at home.

GEORGE MACDONALD

Wind and Silver

Greatly shining,
The autumn moon floats in the sky;
And the fish-ponds shake their backs and flash
    their dragon scales
As she passes over them.

AMY LOWELL

Dreams

Here we are all, by day; by night we are hurled
By dreams, each one into a several world.

ROBERT HERRICK

Inside our Dreams

Where do people go to when they die?
Somewhere down below or in the sky?
'I can't be sure,' said Grandad, 'but it seems,
They simply set up home inside our dreams.'

JEANNE WILLIS

A Clear Midnight

This is thy hour, O Soul, thy free flight into the
  wordless,
Away from books, away from art, the day erased,
  the lesson done,
Thee fully forth emerging, silent, gazing,
  pondering the themes thou lovest best,
Night, sleep, death and the stars.

WALT WHITMAN

Index of Titles and First Lines

First lines are in italic

84

Acknowledgements

Basho: 'Summer Grasses' from *On Love and Barley: Haiku of Basho* translated by Lucien Stryk (Penguin Classics, 1985), copyright © Lucien Stryk 1985, reprinted by permission of Penguin Books Ltd.

Hilaire Belloc: 'Lord Finchley' from *Cautionary Verses*, copyright © Estate of Hilaire Belloc 1970, and 'The Early Morning' from *Complete Verse*, copyright © The Estate of Hilaire Belloc 1896, 1897, 1899, 1907, 1911, 1930, both reprinted by permission of PFD on behalf of the Estate of Hilaire Belloc.

N. M. Bodecker: 'Radish' and 'Small Rains' from *Snowman Sniffles* (1983), copyright © 1983 N. M. Bodecker, reprinted by permission of the publishers, Faber & Faber Ltd and Margaret K. McElderry Books, an imprint of Simon & Schuster Children's Publishing Division.

Louise Bogan: 'Solitary Observation Brought Back from a Sojourn in Hell' from *The Blue Estuaries*, copyright © 1968 by Louise Bogan, copyright © renewed 1996 by Ruth Limmer, reprinted by permission of the publisher, Farrar, Straus & Giroux, LLC.

Edmund Blunden: translation of 'A Maltese Dog' from the Greek of Tymnes in *From the Greek* (Clarendon Press), reprinted by permission of PFD on behalf of the Estate of Edmund Blunden.

Sandy Brownjohn: 'The Fall-Out' from *Both Sides of the Cat Flap*, reprinted by permission of the publishers, Hodder & Stoughton Ltd.

Elizabeth Coatsworth: 'March' from *Summer Green* (Macmillan, 1948), copyright 1948 by Macmillan Publishing Company, © renewed 1976 Elizabeth Coatsworth: copyright holder not traced.

John Corben: 'In the Eggs...' and 'Harlech Castle' from Michael Harrison: *Junk Mail* (OUP, 1993), reprinted by permission of Michael Harrison.

Po Chu-I: 'Ease' translated by Arthur Waley from *Chinese Poems* (George Allen & Unwin, 1946) reprinted by permission of John Robinson for the Arthur Waley Estate.

Walter de la Mare: 'Napoleon' and 'And So To Bed' from *The Complete Poems of Walter de la Mare* (Faber, 1969, USA 1970), reprinted by permission of The Literary Trustees of Walter de la Mare and The Society of Authors as their representative.

Emily Dickinson: 'The Sun and Fog Contested' and 'They Might Not Need Me' from *The Poems of Emily Dickinson* edited by Ralph W. Franklin (The Belknap Press of Harvard University Press), copyright © 1998 by the President and Fellows of Harvard College, copyright © 1951, 1955, 1979 by the President and Fellows of Harvard College, reprinted by permission of the publishers and the Trustees of Amherst College.

Berlie Doherty: 'Trees' from *Walking on Air* (Hodder & Stoughton), reprinted by permission of David Higham Associates.

Richard Edwards: 'When I was Three' and 'The Blue Room' from *The Word Party* (Lutterworth, 1986), reprinted by permission of the author.

U. A. Fanthorpe: 'The Relief of Myopia' and 'Our Dog Chasing Swifts', copyright © U. A. Fanthorpe 1988, first published in Michael Harrison: *Splinters* (OUP 1988), reprinted by permission of the author.

John Fenniman: 'At the Land's End', 'The Poet's Cat', and 'In the Graveyard', first published in this collection by permission of Michael Harrison.

Simon Forest: 'Butterfly' first published in Michael Harrison: *Junk Mail* (OUP 1993), reprinted by permission of Michael Harrison.

Robert Frost: 'Beyond Words', 'Bravado', and 'The Secret Sits' from *The Poetry of Robert Frost* edited by Edward Connery Lathem (Jonathan Cape), copyright 1942 by Robert Frost, © 1970, 1975 by Lesley Frost Ballantyne, copyright 1947, 1969 by Henry Holt and Co., reprinted by permission of the Random House Group Ltd and Henry Holt and Company, LLC.

John Fuller: 'The Butterfly' from *Come Aboard and Sail Away: Collected Poems for Children* (Salamander Press, 1983), reprinted by permission of the author.

Roy Fuller: 'After Breakfast' from *Seen Grandpa Lately* (Deutsch, 1972), reprinted by permission of John Fuller.

Esther Valck Georges: 'Alley Cat' from *Alley Cat* (Doubleday & Co.): copyright holder not traced.

Robert Graves: 'Love Without Hope' from *Complete Poems*, Volume 2 (1997), reprinted by permission of the publisher, Carcanet Press Ltd.

Ivor Gurney: 'April Gale' and 'If I walked Straight Slap' from *Collected Poems* edited by P. J. Kavanagh (OUP, 1982, new edition Carcanet) reprinted by permission of the publisher, Carcanet Press Ltd.

John Hegley: 'On Bonfire Night' from *Glad to Wear Glasses* (1995), reprinted by permission of the publisher, Andre Deutsch Ltd.

Russell Hoban: 'The Tin Frog' from *The Pedalling Man* (Heinemann, 1968), reprinted by permission of David Higham Associates.

A. E. Housman: 'Infant Innocence (The Grizzly Bear...)' and 'Here Dead Lie We' from *The Collected Poems of A. E. Housman*, copyright 1936 by Barclays Bank Ltd, copyright © 1964 by Robert E. Symons, copyright © 1965 by Henry Holt and Co., reprinted by permission of The Society of Authors as the literary representative of the Estate of A. E. Housman

Patricia Hubbell: 'Shadows' from *Catch Me a Wind* (Atheneum), copyright © 1968, 1996 Patricia Hubbell, reprinted by permission of Marian Reiner for the author.

X. J. Kennedy: 'Bee' from *Did Adam Name the Vinegaroon?* (David R. Godine, 1982), copyright © 1982 by X. J. Kennedy, reprinted by permission of Curtis Brown Ltd, New York.

Roger McGough: 'Snow Poem' (Snow and Ice Poems iii) from *Sky in the Pie* (Puffin, 1983), copyright © 1983, reprinted by permission of PFD on behalf of Roger McGough.

Hugo Majer: 'Spring' from Michael Harrison: *Junk Mail* (OUP, 1993), reprinted by permission of Michael Harrison.

88